MODEL
HISTORICAL AIRCRAFT

BARBARA CURRY

MODEL HISTORICAL AIRCRAFT

**ILLUSTRATIONS BY
ANNE CANEVARI GREEN**

Franklin Watts
New York | London | Toronto | Sydney | 1982
A First Book

Special thanks to Mr. Robert Calandra
of Polk's Hobby Department Store.

Cover photograph: A model of the SPAD fighter plane
flown by Captain "Eddie" Rickenbacker in WW I.

Cover photo and photographs on pp. 14 and 17
by Ginger Giles. Photograph on p. 29 courtesy of
The Smithsonian Institution.

Library of Congress Cataloging in Publication Data

Curry, Barbara A.
Model historical aircraft.
(A First book)
Includes Index.
Summary: Gives instructions on choosing
and assembling models of aircraft,
building a hangar, and acquiring the
necessary supplies. Also includes a brief
history of real aircraft emphasizing
those that are successful as models.
1. Airplanes—Models—Juvenile literature.
(1. Airplanes—Models.
2. Models and modelmaking) I. Title.
TL770.C873   629.133'1   82-4779
ISBN 0-531-04465-3   AACR2

CONTENTS

MODEL
HISTORICAL AIRCRAFT

CHAPTER 1

GETTING OFF
THE GROUND

Have you ever felt a stir of excitement or a twinge of envy when suddenly, way up, you see a jet and its wake of vapor trails? Can you believe that less than eighty years ago the first motorized, piloted flight went only 120 feet (36.6 m) and lasted 12 seconds? Yet for its day and what it meant to the world, that flight was pretty exciting, too!

Building historical models is a great way to experience aviation's past, present, and future. You can recreate the thrills of flying and make history an adventure! From ground zero you're in the pilot's seat in more ways than one. Not only do you choose what you want to "fly," but it's up to you to take a lot of assorted materials and create it. You add your own touches, and finally you roll out your dream machine for all to admire.

This gratifying, I-did-it-myself feeling is one of the main reasons model building is so popular. You'll find lots of buddies. Other hobbies, like collecting things, are rewarding and fun, but they usually ask less of you and more of your budget.

NOT FOR BOYS ONLY

Since women have been in on aviation from the beginning, why shouldn't they be involved now? They may not have been on the designing side, but they sure took to daredevilry. Eliza Garnerin of France parachuted from a balloon in 1815. Any number of women did wing-walking and trapeze stunts from early biplanes. Amelia Earhart and Jacqueline Cochran, both Americans, set speed and distance records. A number of American ferry pilots and Russian fighter pilots in World War II were women. So come on, girls, you've got every right to join any group of model builders.

TO SHOW OR TO FLY

There are only two kinds of aircraft models—those that can't fly, called **static models**, and those that can. Static models include the familiar glue-together plastic kits. There are also snap-together kits and the almost-all-assembled kits, which are often prepainted. All of these models, even the least expensive, are accurately scaled. For example, 1 inch (2.5 cm) might stand for 10 feet (3 m). All of these models have clear, realistic details. They are fun to build, and it doesn't take a lot of time to make them into interesting, decorative showpieces.

Another kind of nonflyer you might try, particularly if you like working with wood, is a carved one. Before plastic became popular, there were many kits that contained balsa wood blocks, sheets, plans, and details. You cut, shaped, and sanded the parts, then assembled and painted them. You can still do this by buying balsa pieces at a hobby store and working from plans or pictures in model magazines. A great variety of plans are also for sale.

Building a meant-to-fly model usually requires more care, more time, and closer attention to details and directions. If you're a beginner, it's a good idea to work with a kit. These kits, like the plastic kits, will supply what you need, except glue and paint, to end up with a very fine model. After you've had some practice with these kits, you may want to wing it with a set of plans and materials you can buy on your own.

Models for show and models to fly can give you great satisfaction and enjoyment. And nobody says you can't do both, particularly if you want to specialize in World War II fighter planes or specific types of planes, such as biplanes.

Before you begin, here are a few things to keep in mind. If you have never built models, start simple. But, unlike some other projects where simple can also mean small, simple means just that—not too complicated or too difficult to handle. You are usually better off working in a medium-sized scale. The parts and pieces are easier to find, prepare, and handle for assembling.

One other thought before you are off and flying. There is a glossary in the back of this book. Listed in it are many technical terms used in building model aircraft as well as some of the basic principles of actual flight. Why not check it out now? Then refer to it as you read and later as you build. Knowing the language of aviation will help move your project along faster and make it come out better.

So blow the dust off history and make it really come to life with your models. Prepare for takeoff!

CHAPTER 2

OUTFITTING
YOUR HANGAR

A big advantage to model building is that it takes so little to put yourself in business. You can set up your work area on almost any kind of table, desk, or snack bar. Of course, always protect the top surfaces even if you're only going to make a fast repair or touch up a paint job. Scratches and spills can occur even while you're doing simple tasks, so save yourself some grief. Cover your work area with newspapers or cardboard cut from a box. It's not a bad idea to top these with a plastic sheet. A garbage bag slit open on the side and bottom works fine. There are also specially-designed model drop cloths that you can buy. These have helpful information printed on them.

   Even if you're using a table or a desk, you can buy or make a workboard. This will give you a sturdy, flat surface that can be moved out of the way without disturbing work in progress. Rather than buy one—workboards can be expensive and probably grander than you need—you can easily make one. Cut two pieces of heavy corrugated cardboard the same size. Cut one piece in the same direction as the ribs go. Cut the other piece across the ribs. This makes the two pieces support each other and prevents warping. (See page

6.) Or, go to a lumber dealer and get a piece of ¼-inch (.6-cm) plywood about 2 feet (.6 m) by 3 feet (.9 m) or larger. Since a specific size isn't needed, ask if there are any scrap pieces. Leftovers are usually much cheaper.

If you plan to build models other than plastic ones, you will want to cover your workboard with something that will make pinning down easier and will hold the pins securely. Good choices for this job are smooth-surfaced home insulating or acoustical ceiling materials that come in sheets or panels. Available at lumberyards and housewares' stores, they are not expensive, and they last a long time.

A **hobby** or **work knife**, sometimes called a razor blade knife, is a must. A holder of some sort is the only safe way to use a blade this sharp. *Never* use a bare blade. One slip can cause a serious cut before you even know it.

The makers of the plastic models suggest you cut the many model pieces apart rather than snapping them with your fingers. You can also use the blade to scrape off any flashings (the rough, unwanted edges caused by the forming process). If you are working with wood, the knife is perfect for cutting, shaping, and shaving. Blades for the holder come in various shapes, so you can buy the right blade for your project. The best is a hobby knife like the one shown. It costs a bit more, but it's specifically designed for model building. Also, the blades can be sharpened and used again and again.

Scissors are also necessary. They have a way of getting lost, so it really is better to buy your own than to borrow. Look for the sturdy, slightly curved kind that are used to cut finger- and toenails. The shape and the sharpness are ideal for cutting out decorative details, small decals, and the tissue and fabric used to cover flyers.

Almost any **glue**, also called **cement,** will do for joining parts. Some kinds are considerably better than others. Good candidates are those that are transparent before and after drying. They are fast dryers and offer a secure, strong bond.

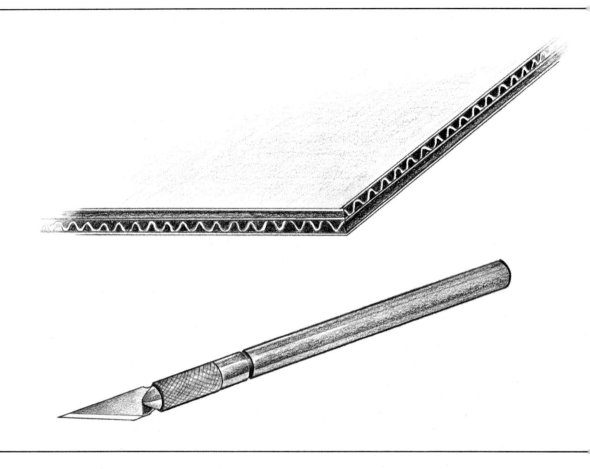

Above: cross section of cardboard layers
Below: hobby knife

So-called hobby glues are sometimes the same as less expensive household types, or they are the instant kinds originally designed for more advanced models. While these instant glues are very good, they work almost too fast for the beginner. Get a little building practice before you try them. Whichever you use, be sure to cap tightly. These glues are inflammable, and they evaporate and harden very quickly.

When you're ready to start assembling your model, you'll find that a sheet of **waxed paper** is a good cover for your work surface. Glue and paint don't readily "take" to wax. This means freshly glued or painted sections that are set down won't stick to the paper.

Flat wooden toothpicks are good glue spreaders for all kinds of models. They are easy to come by and inexpensive. You can "brush" glue on large areas with the wide end. The narrow end works well on smaller parts and in tight, hard-to-get-at places. A toothpick also can neatly clean up any unwanted glue that oozes out along seams and between pieces.

If you are building aircraft other than plastic or solid non-flyers, you will need **model** or **T pins**. The common **straight pin** and **pushpin** can also be used, but because of its length and "handle" the T pin is easier to work with. These pins hold glued wood, cloth, paper, and plastic repairs. For any type of model finishing, pins are perfect for picking up and placing small details like insignia, marking, and numbers. They make it easier for you to see what you're doing and they help keep your fingers and the model free from glue smears.

Very fine **sandpaper** or the fine side of a fingernail emery board should be used to smooth rough spots and round edges. Too coarse a grain will dig in and leave scratch marks.

Two kinds of **tape, masking** and **clear**, are handy to have. Masking tape is used to hold the larger cemented sections of plastic models together and keep them from shifting until they dry. Clear tape is most often used when you are painting your model. It can protect details and certain areas that you do not wish to cover with the paint you are using at the time. The clear tape is best for this job because it can be cut easily and accurately with a hobby knife. You can also see exactly where and what you want to cut. The tape will come off cleanly if you lightly fingerprint the sticky side before you put it on the area to be masked. Instead of tape, you can use an easy-to-remove masking liquid that can be painted on. This is relatively new and may have to be mail-ordered from larger hobby outlets.

To finish up your model in style, you'll need **paint**, or **dope**, and **brushes**. Choosing the proper paint sometimes can be confusing. When you see a label that says "for models," you may think that means all models, but it doesn't necessarily. So be sure your paint chemistry matches your project. Until you're more experienced it's a good idea to follow the suggestions from the model manufacturer. Fortunately, almost all the kits now have a list of the paint and other extras you'll need printed on the outside of the package. A manufacturer will more often than not suggest his brand of paint. Actually, the *kind* of paint that you need (such as acrylic or tempera) is more important than the brand. Remember not to buy more paint than you need.

You could possibly save money by buying such basic colors as white, black, and silver in large sizes. But unless you are practically running a model factory, the less-than-an-ounce sizes are better. This paint really covers a lot of territory. Paint sets that offer ranges of eight to twelve shades are a good value. Any paint will work on the solid carved balsa wood models, but the water soluble ones are easier to clean up and store. For some unknown reason, **dope** is and always has been the name for the paint for fabric- and paper-covered models. Dope was used on the cloth coverings of early aircraft before their "skins" were metal. Dope does more than provide a flashy paint job. It strengthens, tightens, and waterproofs whatever material it covers.

Experienced modelers use plastic sheeting in almost any hue, instead of dope-covered materials. Plastic sheeting does a super covering job, but it's expensive and needs a special heat-sealing tool. Put this item on hold for now.

Before we discuss brushes, something should be said for and against spray paint. There is no doubt that when properly applied, spray paint gives the smoothest, most professional-looking finish. However, it takes a bit of practice to avoid heavy spurts and thin spots. Also, the mist of spray seems to travel farther and faster than the speed of sound. Before attempting a spray job, cover everything in sight with newspapers; then add more newspapers for insurance.

Brushes are ideal because they give you more control. You can paint at your own speed and in the direction you want. You'll probably want a couple of brush sizes and shapes (pointed and flat). No matter which suits your project, buy the best brush you can afford. Cheap brushes often shed their hair just where you don't want them to—in the paint or on the model. They also tend to leave more brush marks and won't form a good point or edge for painting a clean line.

If you don't take good care of a brush, you'll waste your money and spoil the brush for future use. When you're finished with it, paint out as much leftover paint as you can on a newspaper or paper towel. Then dip the brush in the solvent (paint thinner or water) that's right for the paint you are using. Paint out again and again, if necessary, on clean paper until the color is mostly gone. Then use mild soap and warm water to finish the cleaning. Shake the brush dry, and reshape it if you have to. Dry and store the brush either on its side or handle end down in a glass or cup.

Many model builders like to use a brush for gluing, too. But never use the same brush for both.

MATERIALS REQUIRED TO COMPLETE
AN UNASSEMBLED KIT

Glue   Use cement available in liquid or tube form

Paint   #123 Red Spray (or #456 Red Brush-on)
          #9101 Glosscote

Knife   Good, sharp hobby knife (#11 blade)

Tape   Clear

OPTIONAL SUPPLIES

Brushes   #123 Nylon
          #2 Red Sable Artist's

Other   #123 Silver
          #456 Black
          #789 Tan
          #012 Glosscote
          #345 Thinner
          #678 Gray, Black Tempera (water based)

These, then, are the basic tools, materials, and equipment you'll need to set up your first hangar. As you go from one model to another, you'll find your own shortcuts, other methods, and new items that will help fill out your new hobby.

One thing has not been mentioned so far, and it's something you can't buy. It's free, but most important: **patience**. You may be able to afford the fanciest tools and the most expensive kits, but unless you have patience you'll be disappointed with what you build. Sometimes this isn't easy. It's only natural to want your model to be just like the pictured beauty in no time flat. You may be tempted to do such things as over-gluing to make parts stick together faster, blowing on parts to speed up drying time, or skipping over a direction or two. Resist the rush. Each step has its own reason, fun, and challenge. And when your small craft comes out looking like its real, high-flying big sister, you'll be happy you took the time.

CHAPTER 3

MODEL KITS

WHERE TO BUY KITS

When the molded plastic kits were introduced some years ago, model building became a possibility for almost everyone. There are many kinds of models and kits to choose from. Even the smallest variety shops know the value of having a model section.

Of course, the best places to shop for the widest range are the larger stores that have a hobby/craft department or the specialized hobby/craft businesses. Besides kits, these outlets also carry additional materials and supplies such as hobby knives, paints, and extra parts that you might need. Some of these places have mail-order catalogs that offer hundreds of items. You can buy anything from elaborate kits to wheels, even if you can't get to the store.

Other sources, particularly good for historical model aircraft, are the gift shops of museums devoted to aviation and science. Also, mail-order catalogs that specialize in science or leisure time usually have some interesting selections.

Never to be overlooked, if you are having trouble finding what you want, are the ads in model magazines. These are practically supermarkets for model builders.

You will find that most kits you buy have information about and an order form for new or favorite models.

WHAT MODEL KIT TO BUY

Even if you are concentrating on historical model aircraft, that is no handicap when it comes to the variety and number of kits available. If anything, it sometimes seems that *all* model kits are historic. However, the ones you'll probably be most interested in are called **antiques** or **classics.** Antiques are historic because they are old or curious-looking and belong to the very first days of flying. Classics usually signify aircraft (old or new) that made a breakthrough in aviation. Or, they are aircraft that featured an outstanding performance or difference of some sort.

There are some things to remember when selecting the kit that you want to buy. First, since the kits are sealed either by an over-all wrap or around the box edges, don't buy one that has been opened. Some vital parts may be missing. Second, don't open a box to take a peek! Third, even though the action pictures on the outside of the box are glorious, they are a bit of a come-on. You'll be hard put to match perfectly the pictures at first. And don't forget that the people who build or draw these replicas have logged a lot of flight time learning how.

PLASTIC KITS FOR SHOW ONLY

Unfortunately, even when the costs are the same, some kits are not as good as others, inside or out. You'll soon get to know which are which. But for starters, look for kits that provide information about additional materials you might need to complete your model. Although sometimes these suggestions do tend to sell you those supplies made by the kit's manufacturer, they are helpful.

A plastic for-show-only kit,
the classic *Spirit of St. Louis*.

The quality of a kit becomes apparent, of course, when you open the box and go to work. Don't be too quick to blame yourself if you have trouble following the directions or if some parts and pieces are flimsy. You'll be able to manage OK—but make a mental note not to buy that brand of kit again. Fortunately, this poor quality is happening less and less, even in the inexpensive models.

Assembling your model will be much easier if you follow a few guidelines. Read and reread the directions before you start. It's true that most kits, even rather involved ones, generally follow the same steps. But there are differences, particularly in small details, and if you miss these you may have to spend a lot of time and trouble on a problem that never should have occurred.

While the parts are still hooked together on what is called a **sprue**, identify them using the plans. If you are going to paint, now is the time. Chances are you'll get a better paint job if you wash the parts in soap and warm water. Rinse well and allow them to dry completely. Then apply the paint, brushing the larger areas in one direction. This will help produce a smoother coating with few, if any, brush marks. Be patient! Let the paint dry thoroughly. Then use your hobby knife to cut and separate the pieces. Cut or scrape off any flashings. Fit the parts together before you glue. If the fit isn't a good one because of uneven plastic, or if you notice paint on the edges to be joined (glue won't take on painted surfaces), scrape the edges clean. Keep trying until you get a snug fit. This also gives you practice in placing parts accurately, which lowers the chance of smearing glue where you don't want it. One word about glue: a light, even coating is all you need. Too much will just ooze out and is messy to remove.

With your first models, be content with getting your "baby" as close as you can to the picture on the box. As you gain building experience, your models will look better and better.

Soon though, if you're like most model buffs, you'll want to try the more complicated optional details and finer finishing touches. You'll want to make your model look real rather than like it just came off the assembly line. For instance, add exhaust marks from an engine, splash marks on the landing gear, or even bullet holes in the tail of your Sopwith Camel. Just because you begin with a somewhat standard nonflying model doesn't mean you have to ground your imagination.

FLYERS

Flying models not only look like the historical originals, they are built from the inside out like the real ones. You'll be dealing with different materials—balsa wood in strips and sheets, plastic, and wire, used separately or in combination with paper, fabric, and plastic sheeting.

Some of these kits have shortcomings. In some cases, the information on the box may be scantier than the information on the for-show-only kits. This may be because the manufacturer thinks you know more than you do. There are many beginners like you, so don't be afraid to ask questions. Most hobby dealers know their business and want to help. Here is some information to get you started:

Prefabricated parts means that some of the trickier or more involved assembling has already been done.

Printed die-cut parts means that the pieces have been cut for you by the manufacturer. You may have to do some sanding and finishing.

Printed parts leaves the cutting out up to you. These parts are clearly outlined and identified, but they are fitted very close together on the balsa sheets. Be sure your knife blade is as sharp as it can be for this precise work.

The plans and directions are more complicated, so read instructions and check out your raw materials before starting. Unlike the plans with plastic model kits, which are for direc-

A balsa-wood flyer kit for
a popular antique plane.

tions only, here you actually form the main sections of your craft directly on the plans.

To insure that your model will eventually fly, you need an absolutely flat surface (see pages 4 and 5) to work on. Any warping or variation of the true lines of the framework can affect flight performance.

Since you are working on the plans, put waxed paper over them and fasten both securely to your work surface.

Most of these kits promise more, so they also have to deliver more. You'll find the quality consistently good. Your main problems may be the technical terms and the tendency to cut short directions so they will fit in small spaces on the plans. Most often you are guided quite well through the basic construction and assembly. However, some kit instructions treat the covering of the frame very briefly and go directly to finishing details such as paint shades, decorations, numbers and letters.

Covering the frame is not quite as easy as it sounds. Never "wrap" a model. Covering the frame is done a section at a time. Cut the paper or fabric slightly larger than and approximately the shape of the section to be covered. Lightly glue or dope a long edge of the frame that the material will touch. On a wing it would be the trailing edge. Press the covering in place. Allow it to dry. Then glue or dope the opposite edge and fit the covering over, pulling as tight as you can without causing too much strain. With flat pieces such as the tail, pinning down the material first may help. After the glue has dried, trim the edges of the material as close as possible to the frame. To tighten the covering, spray it with a fine mist of water. You can use a household cleaner spray bottle.

Finally, paint on one coat of dope as an undercoat. Allow this to dry completely. Then, very lightly sand any ragged edges or rough spots before you put on the finishing coat.

Until you have built a few of these models, try to resist spending money on the more glamorous, advanced "ultras." (It is hard—some of these are tempting.) Many kits and fancy extras are designed for "old hands" who are very experienced model builders. It's wise to wait until you've had some practice before you try these.

To avoid disappointment, regard your first model or two as trainers. Even real pilots have to go through this kind of training period before they earn their wings. Don't be too upset if the model you've built doesn't quite match the perfect model pictured on the box and in your imagination. It didn't come easy for aviation pioneers either. Everyone has to start somewhere. So let's start mixing the past with the present, a bit of fun with some ideas and glue . . . and up, up and away!

CHAPTER 4

BUILD YOUR OWN
HALL OF FAME

Now's your chance to relive those adventures in air history. How you do it is up to you. You can start where the air pioneers did, with balloons, and work your way forward in time and upward in space. Maybe you'd rather concentrate on one time period such as the dashing wonder-how-they-flew era of World War I. Or you can build special kinds of aircraft, such as jets. Whatever your choice, you'll find more than enough to keep you busy and happy for hours.

BALLOONS

Wild ideas and experiments in aviation date back at least to Leonardo da Vinci, the Italian artist and inventor, in 1513. But credit for opening the air age goes to two French brothers, Joseph and Étienne Montgolfier. In June 1783 they sent up a balloon made of linen and paper. It was lifted by the heat from a wood and straw fire! By the end of the same year, the first gas-filled (hydrogen) balloon was designed by Frenchman Jacques A.C. Charles. It was amazingly like a modern balloon, with rubberized fabric, a basket, valves to control the gas, a ballast, and even a barometer. It flew 27 miles (43 km) with two people aboard.

Balloons were the center of attention at shows and fairs, offering rides to the daring. They also were used as launching pads for fireworks displays and the first parachute drops. Balloons were soon discovered by the military and were used as sky-high spies.

For many years, balloons took a back seat to speedier aircraft and were used mostly for gathering scientific information. Recently, however, ballooning for fun has made a popular comeback.

You can make a balloon every bit as fancy as the old-fashioned ones from everyday items. You can copy from illustrations or let your imagination loose and create your own. All you need to make a balloon is a globe with lines that connect to the passenger basket. Look around!

For the balloon part, you can use a real balloon. After the balloon is inflated, decorate it with marker pens, decals, or cut-outs pasted on. How about smooth-surfaced balls such as ping-pong balls, rubber balls of all sizes, or even beach balls if you think big? Styrofoam balls, Christmas ornaments, and Japanese lanterns are all good candidates. In fact, almost anything that is round can work, but the lighter the better.

If you are going to hang your balloon, use clear plastic mylar or heavy sewing thread or string for the lines. Depending what you use for the balloon, you may be able to attach the lines directly by gluing them on. If this isn't possible, you may need to create a stop of some sort (see diagram) to keep the balloon in place.

If you want the "netted look" that many balloons feature, use ordinary onion sacking.

If you are going to stand your balloon, the lines will have to be rigid and strong enough to support the weight of the

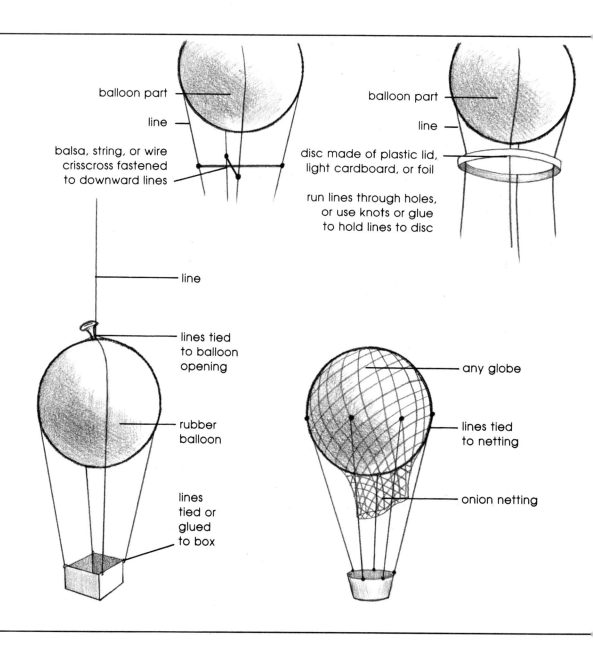

balloon part

line

balsa, string, or wire
crisscross fastened
to downward lines

balloon part

line

disc made of plastic lid,
light cardboard, or foil

run lines through holes,
or use knots or glue
to hold lines to disc

line

lines tied
to balloon
opening

rubber
balloon

lines
tied or
glued
to box

any globe

lines tied
to netting

onion netting

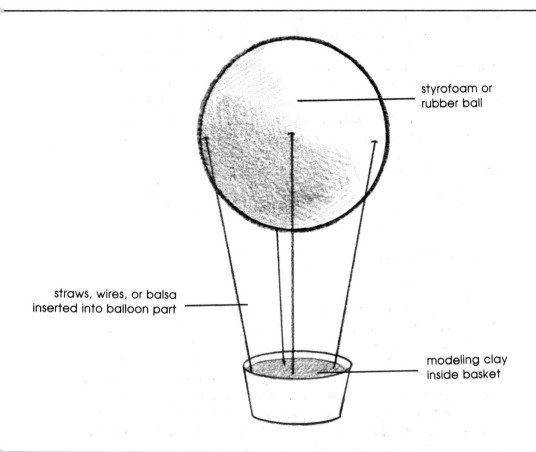

styrofoam or
rubber ball

straws, wires, or balsa
inserted into balloon part

modeling clay
inside basket

DO-IT-YOURSELF BALLOONS
Left: hanging balloons
Above: standing balloon

balloon. Some possibilities are stiff wire, soda straws, pipe cleaners, drink stirrers, balsa sticks, and small dowels.

For the basket, just about any small, unlidded, square box or round container will do. Be sure its size is in scale with the rest of the model. Paint or cover the outside as you wish. You can paint on ballast sandbags for realistic detail.

If you want your balloon to fly, get a small pressurized can of helium. Helium is a lighter-than-air, safe, nontoxic gas. It Is fairly expensive, but you can stretch it by using your breath to blow the balloon up halfway and then adding the helium. The more helium you use, the more the lift. Remember to use an anchor line, or it's bye-bye balloon!

LIGHTER THAN AIR

Blimps

Often, the flight path of the balloon depended on which way the wind was blowing. From the beginning, all sorts of controls were tried—even those that resembled boat oars! The first successful propeller-driven flight was in 1852. A short time later, the blimp and then the dirigible, or rigid airship, were developed. Both of these are powered by engine-driven propellers and steered with rudders. They are filled with a lighter-than-air gas—originally the highly flammable hydrogen, later the safe nonflammable helium.

The blimp is basically a sausage-shaped balloon. In its earlier days it was shaped by the pressure of the gas inside it. Today's blimps, often seen at sports events, have a rigid keel that helps them keep their shape and stability. Although their function these days is mostly commercial, they were used on antisubmarine and coastal patrols in past wars.

You can make your own blimp model from a long party balloon. Use thin cardboard or paper to make the gondola

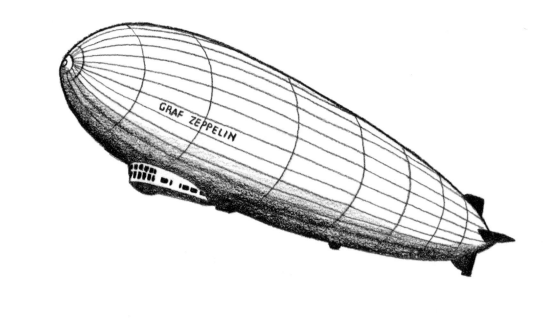

Graf Zeppelin

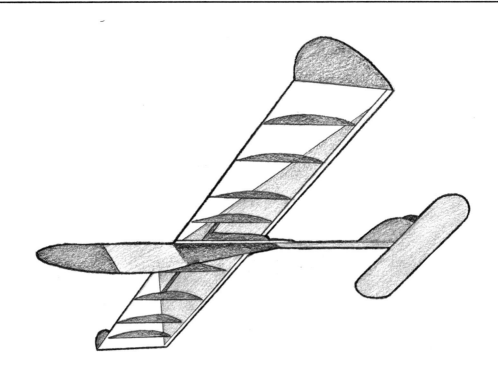

**Model glider
built from kit**

(cabin) and fins. An inexpensive novelty blimp kit (for show only) is great fun.

Dirigibles

The dirigible was a rigid airship, meaning that its skin was stretched over a framework of lightweight metal. The gas it was filled with was only for lift and didn't affect the shape of the ship. The dirigible was believed to be the future of long-distance air travel, but the only ones you'll ever see are in old movies or in aviation history books. They may have been rigid, but they weren't rugged. One of the most famous dirigibles (and one that didn't crash) was the German-built Graf Zeppelin. It traveled 20,000 miles (32,000 km) around the world in 1929. For all practical purposes, the age of the dirigible ended with the fiery crash of the hydrogen-filled German *Hindenburg* in 1937.

HEAVIER THAN AIR

Gliders

Gliders use only air currents to make them fly. The first successful glider flight with a person aboard was in 1849 in England. The glider was designed by Sir George Caley. The takeoff was managed by towing the glider downhill into a light breeze.

Another pioneer, Otto Lilienthal, firmly believed true flight could be achieved by flapping wings like the birds. He was wrong, of course, but his idea to use the pilot's body as the fuselage, or central portion, of the glider was the beginning of hang gliding as we know it today.

Glider models are for flying. You can build them with kits that range from the smaller balsa or plastic trainers to those with 11-foot (3.3-m) wingspans!

Flying Machines

Gliders constantly improved. All they needed were engines that were light enough yet powerful enough to produce lift. The Wright brothers had studied other gliders and flight principles and had flown their own gliders. After much study, and many tests, Orville and Wilbur Wright built their own engine-powered glider. The world changed forever in twelve seconds on December 17, 1903, when the *Flyer I*, with Orville Wright as pilot, flew 120 feet (36.6 m).

Kits for show and/or for flying are available for the *Flyer I* and all of the aircraft on the following pages.

As with balloons, the military realized the importance of aircraft. During World War I, the sky became a battlefield. Individual Allied and German fighter planes fought each other in one-on-one dogfights. There was a sort of comradeship, unheard of before or since, between these daring enemy pilots. One of the most famous combat pilots was the Red Baron.

Rittmeister Manfred von Richthofen, or the Red Baron, was the greatest ace of World War I. At the time of his death (in action) he was credited with eighty victories. The story goes that he flew his own all-red plane. Actually, he flew several planes, some all-red, some partially red, of two types—the Albatross D. III and the Fokker Dr. I.

After World War I, many warplanes were used to carry cargo, mail, and passengers. (It was a little breezy in the open cockpits!) Many adventurous pilots took the planes "barnstorming" to perform stunts and mock air battles. They thrilled thousands and introduced them to the air age.

The Germans and Japanese had lots of "practice" in air combat during wars in Spain and China. So, they had a tremendous advantage at the start of World War II. As the war went on, however, the Allies gradually gained air superiority. During the war, aircraft developments came fast and

**The plane that started it all:
The Wright *Flyer I* taking off.**

furiously. Theories became realities as the jet engine replaced the piston and the propeller became history.

Out of World War II came prop jets, turbo jets, rocket engines, speeds faster than sound, and heights literally out of this world. It is impossible to list the hundreds of aircraft, almost all classics in one way or another, which made or are making aviation history. Two that led the way are the Bell X-I and the Concorde SST.

Next to its sleek, fast, and high-flying sisters, the helicopter looks awkward and slow. It was first designed in 1500 by Leonardo da Vinci. The helicoptor wasn't actually built until hundreds of years later.

During the Korean war in 1950 it proved its worth. Now helicopters are used to report traffic, fly rescue missions, and carry troops, supplies, and passengers. The helicopter is the workhorse of aviation.

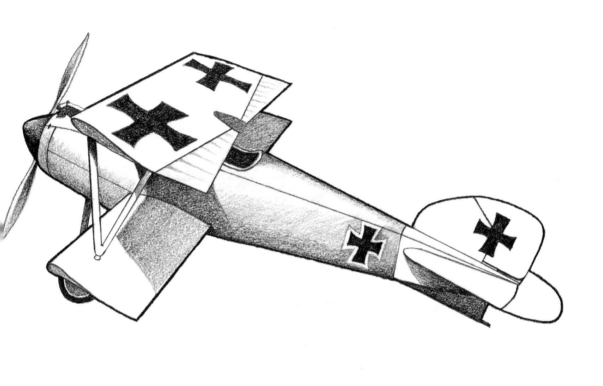

Here's a typical Albatross D III. It is like the many that
were in the squadrons of the Red Baron's "Flying Circus"
(named after their planes' many different colors and designs).
You, too, can make your own plane with unique decorations.
The national symbol (the Bismarck Cross) on the tail is
required, but wings, body, colors, and extras are up to you.

This Fokker Dr. 1 was a favorite of the Red Baron.
It is a rare triplane, a design that was developed
by the early peacetime pioneers.

The British Sopwith Camel is the most celebrated
member of the Sopwith family. Other Sopwiths
of that time served in the navy; the Pup made
the first landing on a ship under way and then
went on to serve on the first aircraft carrier.

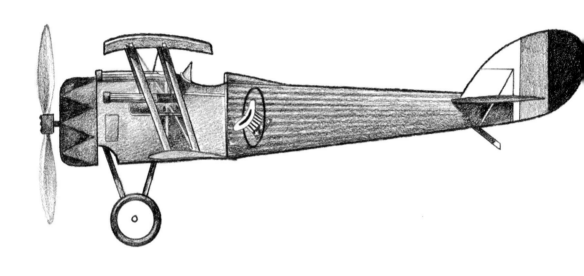

The Nieuport was the aircraft used for the first
American patrol action in the war. American ace
"Eddie" Rickenbacker and the "hat-in-a-ring"
squadron symbol are connected with this aircraft.

The Curtiss JN series planes, widely known as
"Jennies," were designed to be used as military
trainers. They began the first airmail service
between New York and Washington in May 1918.

Two Douglas World Cruiser biplanes made
the first successful round-the-world flight
in 1924. They took off from Seattle, Washington,
on April 6 and returned on September 8.

The *Spirit of St. Louis*, piloted by Charles
Lindbergh, made the first nonstop solo flight
across the Atlantic Ocean in May 1927.

The DC-3 is probably the most famous airliner
in history. First flown in 1935, it joined the
U.S. Air Corps in 1941 as the Skytrain transport,
which carried troops and equipment. This amazing
aircraft is still very much on the scene today.

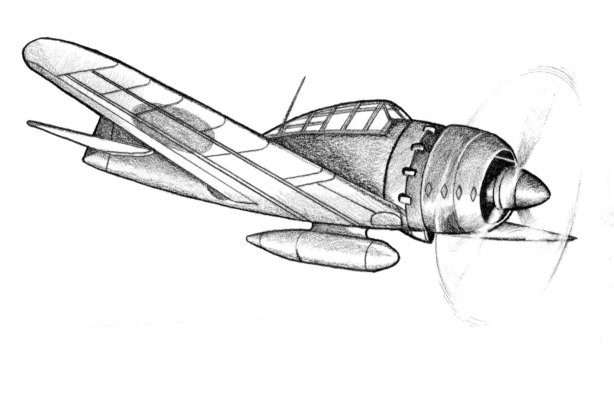

The Mitsubishi A6M Zero was the famous Japanese
fighter plane flown by kamikaze pilots. It also
was the first Japanese plane with an enclosed
cockpit and retractable landing gear.

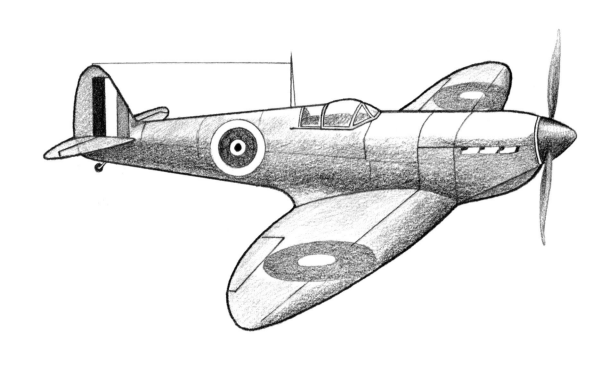

The Spitfire and the Battle of Britain are forever linked
in heroic terms. From August to October 1940, Britain's
Royal Air Force, although outnumbered, destroyed
2,300 German aircraft and lost only 900 of its own.

The B-17s were the first of America's famous
Flying Fortresses. In whatever version, they bristled
with guns. By the end of the war, 12,731 Flying
Fortresses had rolled off the production line.

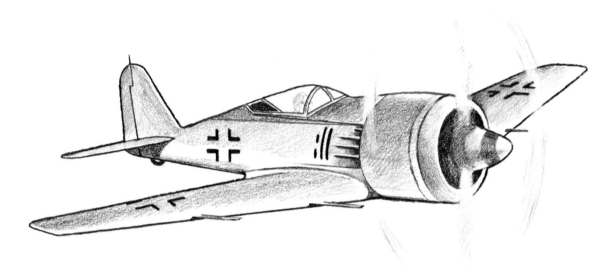

One of the classic German fighters, the Focke-Wulf FW 190,
provided a protective "air umbrella" for the Channel dash
of two German battleships and one cruiser in early 1942.

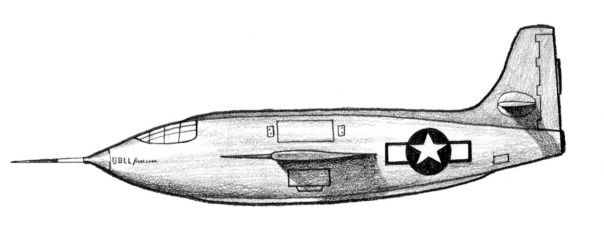

The Bell X-I is usually considered to be second only
to the Wright brothers' *Flyer I* in historical importance.
In 1947, piloted by USAF Captain Charles Yeager,
it broke the sound barrier.

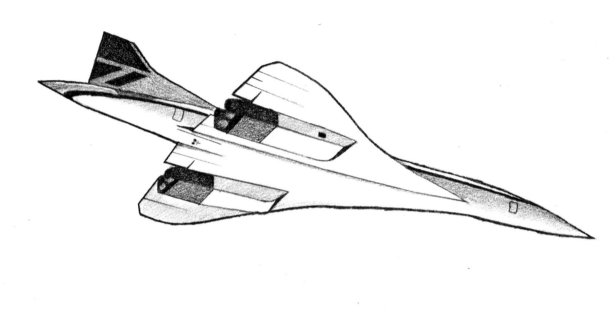

Although the Russians were the first to fly
an SST (SuperSonic Transport) prototype, the
Anglo-French Concorde opened up this new means
of air travel to commercial passengers.

The Bell Jet Ranger helicopter

CHAPTER 5

ROLLOUT TIME

Rollout means exactly what it says. It's when you roll your new aircraft out of the hangar for the first time. Now you can see, test, and enjoy the results of all your planning, building, and finishing.

After this moment of triumph where does your "baby" go? If it's meant to fly, outdoors is the best place. There you have space and natural air currents, two requirements for successful flights. Smaller gliders can be flown indoors, but all prop-driven planes should be flown outside unless you have access to a large high-ceilinged area such as a school gym or a community arena.

If you have built your model correctly, it should fly well, even if it's a modest one. But just as real aircraft need test flights, trial runs, and a little tinkering, so may yours.

1. Make a preflight check to be as sure as you can that all systems are go. Double-check for any warping or any out-of-line surfaces. You can often correct these faults with steam from a tea kettle. Be careful! Keep your fingers clear of the steam. It can give you a bad burn, fast. Don't hold the part too close or overdo the steam. You can always go back for more. Remove from the steam and test whether you can twist the part gently. When you can, either hold or pin it in the correct position until it is cool and firm.

2. Size is more or less the only difference between your model and real aircraft. Just as pilots do, take off nose first into the wind. If a strong wind is blowing, your model will not have the power to buck it. Don't launch in such winds at all, or you'll be back to the workboard sooner than you think.

3. Take it easy. Your model is not a ball, so don't throw it like one. Let the air currents and motor help you. A too-fast or pushy send-off will build up air resistance and fight the launch. Send off the plane in a slight nose-up position, and try for a smooth, balanced release.

4. There are no special on-the-spot tricks you can perform to break flight records for distance, altitude, or speed. These variables are determined by the design and construction of the aircraft itself. Some adjustments will simply help the plane fly as it is meant to, but won't cause it to break any records.

If you've never tried to fly a model before, it's a good idea to buy an inexpensive glider to learn about common flight problems and experiment on how to correct them.

The glider may take a sharp, curved, downward path, or dive. To correct this, move the wing toward the nose, a touch at a time, if you can. Or, tilt the wing tips up a little; or slightly tilt the stabilizer down; or add weight to the tail. Clay is good for this because you can add or remove small amounts.

When a glider stalls, its flight is wavy. Each wave gets a little deeper, until all forward motion is stopped and the model drops to the ground. If you can, move the wing toward the tail, a touch at a time; or tilt the wing tips down a little; or slightly tip the stabilizer up; or add weight to the nose, again using clay.

Naturally, troubleshooting a more complicated model than a glider can be more difficult and might require some minor construction and adjustments. Try weighting, positioning, and angling your model as you would a glider. If that doesn't work, ask for help. Model builders just love to give advice.

PUT MODELS ON DISPLAY

All your aircraft models, whether they are flyers or not, should have their day in the sun. Even if you don't have lots of room, you can probably make a landing pad on a windowsill, a desk, a cabinet top, or a bookshelf. These spaces almost always work best with the for-show-only models, which usually have a smaller wingspan than flyers.

Don't forget that the setting is an important part of your model display, too! If, for example, your model is the Red Baron's favorite red, set it on or in front of a black or strong blue. Backgrounds can be made with the help of sticky-backed plastic, paint, or even swatches of felt. Look around for color—any number of materials can work.

For an in-flight look, you can mount your models on either pegboard or simple wood blocks. Attach the models by gluing and/or inserting connecting "rods," like wooden dowels, matches (fireplace matches are perfect for extra length), pipe cleaners, even plastic swizzle sticks and straws. To add slight movement and to take advantage of air currents, use balsa sticks or springy wire for mounting.

**Planes mounted on pegboard. Clockwise from top:
Douglas DC-3, Sopwith Camel, Curtiss "Jenny."**

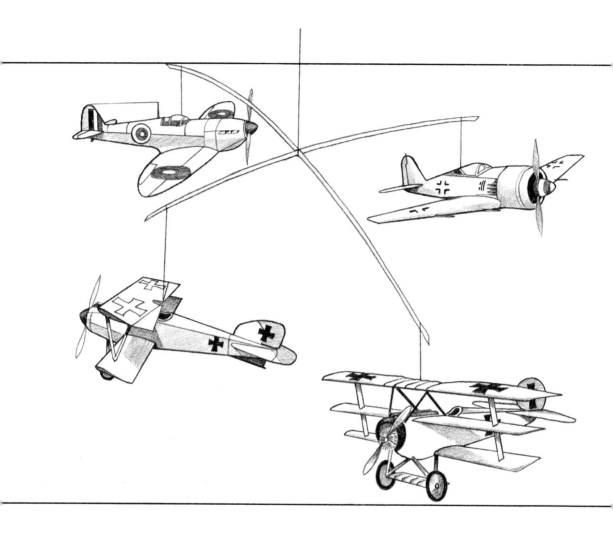

Mobile of warplanes. Clockwise from upper left: Spitfire, Focke-Wulf FW 190, Fokker Dr 1, Albatross D III.

For pegboard mounting, if the angle you're after is a straight-on side view, make the attacher rod slightly longer than the wing. For other angles, like an extreme bank, determine the right length by the widest part of the plane. The idea, of course, is that the attacher doesn't show or shows very little. Depending on the diameter of the attacher, you may have to add a touch of glue or insert a small wedge to get a tight fit in the pegboard hole.

With a block-mounted model, the attacher will show, of course. But you can make it almost invisible by using clear plastic, fine, springy wire, or a balsa stick painted to match the model. You can create a forward-motion effect by curving the wire or balsa stick. Depending on the weight of your plane, the balsa stick may have to be dampened and pinned down until dry to form the curve you want.

For an exciting, realistic display hang your model with a clear plastic line. This works for all models. Since most models, even some big flyers, weigh next to nothing, a spot of glue or a piece of tape is all you need to attach the line to your plane. For heavier models, make a sling or use two lines. For both the light- or heavyweights, allow plenty of line so you can adjust the model to the height you want. Secure the line to the hanging surface with tape or by tying it to a small screw eye or hook.

You can create your own air war or flying formation by making a mobile with two or more planes. You need clear plastic line for the vertical hangers. For the horizontal crossbars that hold the hangers, use wire that's just flexible enough to bend and work with, yet won't sag or droop.

Attach the lines, allowing extra for adjusting. From then on it's trial-and-error balancing. If you have a heavy bomber, try counterbalancing it with two or three light fighters. Try an arrangement on a flat surface, and then hold or temporarily hang the mobile up to see what the free-swinging effect is. One plane may drag the others down or pull them too high and so on. By shifting the models and shortening or lengthening the crossarms and lines, you'll eventually get your dogfight going. And go it will, because these mobiles move with even the slightest breeze.

CHAPTER 6

GET A COPILOT

Model building can be a solo performance, but there are literally thousands of modelers who like to share their fun and experience. Here are some ways you can get in on the action.

• *Join a club.* There are model clubs all over the world, but most of them are small, local, and friendly associations, absolutely dedicated to the wild blue yonder. Your best way to find them is to check with your school, community, or local newspaper. Ask at the place where you buy your kits and materials. Many of these stores, particularly the hobby stores, know about local clubs.

• *Start your own club.* If you can't find a club, or if the one you find is too far away or too advanced, form your own club. (Many clubs have a program for junior modelers, so don't be afraid to ask.)

Look for possible clubmates, especially where you buy your models. Ask the owner for some names, then either write or call about the possibility of getting together.

Another good way to find new flying buddies is to go to a "meet"—and it means exactly what you think it means. It's a place and a time, usually agreed upon beforehand, where model builders can meet to talk, compare, and compete. While most of the models being shown and flown are out of your class for now, you can learn a lot and have fun doing it.

• *Read model magazines.* These are like food for the confirmed model builder. However, they can be somewhat expensive and usually devote most of their pages to very advanced model aircraft. But the ads, special columns for beginners, letters from readers, and general information are great, even if you're not that advanced. Before you subscribe, see which one appeals most to you. Look for copies at your library or single issues at a hobby or magazine store.

Building historical aircraft is a hobby that celebrates the past. In a way it's part of the present too, because almost every year aviation history is being made. There's no other hobby quite like it for mixing the old with the new. So give it a try—if it's the hobby for you, you'll have a friend for life.

NATIONAL ORGANIZATIONS
AND MAGAZINES

The following are not clubs in the usual sense of the word, but they are excellent organizations and good sources of information.

Academy of Model Aeronautics
815 15th Street, N.W.
Washington, D.C. 20005

Yearly membership in the Academy of Model Aeronautics can entitle you to receive their magazine, *Model Aviation*, a newsletter, and other privileges.

National Association of Rocketry
182 Madison Drive
Elizabeth, Pennsylvania 15037

They publish a national rocketry magazine and offer a host of services to model rocket builders.

International Plastic Modelers Society
P.O. Box 2555
Long Beach, California 90801

An international club for static model builders that has local chapters, holds conventions, and publishes a newsletter

Hobby Industry Association of America
319 East 54th Street
Elmwood Park, New Jersey 07407

Subscription and newsstand magazines of interest are:

Flying Models
Carsten Publications Inc.
P.O. Box 700
Newton, New Jersey 07860

International Modeler
P.O. Box 1208
Topanga, California 90290

Model Airplane News
Air Age Inc.
One North Broadway
White Plains, New York 10601

Scale Modeler
Challenge Publications Inc.
7950 Deering Avenue
Canoga Park, California 91304

Aero Modeller
Incorporated with Model Aircraft
Model & Allied Publication, Ltd.
P. O. Box 35, Bridge Street
Hemel Hempstead
Hertfordshire HPI IEE, Great Britain

GLOSSARY

Aero-: a word part (prefix) used to define anything dealing with air or atmosphere, as in *aeronautics*, which means, literally, "sailing in air," and *aerodynamics*, which is a science that deals with the motion of air and other gases.

Aileron: a movable part of a wing used to maintain balance and to bank.

Anhedral: the downward angle of wings in relation to the fuselage.

Balsa: extremely lightweight, flexible wood.

Bank: to turn a plane to the left or right by dropping the corresponding wing.

Bay: any compartment set apart from the rest of the aircraft.

Camber: the curve of a surface or body of a plane.

Cement: used interchangeably with glue, either as a process that permanently binds two or more parts together (verb) or a product that accomplishes that process (noun).

Cockpit: a compartment of a plane for the pilot (crew) and the necessary controls and instruments for flying.

Cowling: the streamlined shell that covers a plane's engine to reduce air resistance.

Dihedral: the upward angle of wings in relation to the fuselage.

Dive: to plunge downward at a steeper angle than a glide.

Dope: a coating applied to paper or fabric to make the material stronger and waterproof.

Drag: any force exerted on a plane that tends to reduce its forward motion.

Elevator: the movable rear end of the horizontal stabilizer, which helps control the pitch of the airplane (nose up/down).

Flap: a hinged section of the wing used to increase lift and decrease speed.

Friction: the resistance caused by the movement of one body against another.

Fuselage: the framework and main section of a plane.

Glider: a motorless aircraft designed to fly by using and taking advantage of natural currents of air; also a fixed-wing aircraft.

Gondola: the part of a balloon, blimp, or dirigible that carries the crew and passengers, if any.

Gravity: the force acting to draw and hold material objects to earth; the attraction a plane must overcome to fly.

Gusset: an angular piece of material fitted into a joint to strengthen it.

Head Wind: a strong movement of air blowing toward a plane that creates resistance and slows flight.

Lift: a force exerted by an airflow that opposes the pull of gravity.

Longeron: a main lengthwise brace in the fuselage.

Longitudinal Axis: the nose-to-tail axis of a plane.

Mach: pronounced "mock"—a unit of speed equal to the speed of sound in air. Mach 1 is about 730 miles (1,168 km) per hour at sea level.

Nose: the prominent front of the fuselage. In single-engine planes it houses the engine.

Propeller: a wooden or metal (can be plastic on models) part, which, when spun by a motor, moves a plane forward; in a helicoptor, it moves vehicle up also.

Prototype: an original aircraft used for experimenting and testing. The results usually lead to production of refined versions of aircraft.

Rib: an arched support that shapes and strengthens a wing surface.

Rudder: a vertical tail part that helps steer a plane.

Sound Barrier: an invisible "wall," marked by unusual vibrations and noises, created when an aircraft comes near the speed of sound.

Spar: any principal longitudinal member of a plane wing.

Sprue: a small plug of metal or plastic that is left over from the molding process. In kits, it is used to hold together and organize various parts, particularly very small ones.

Stall: a loss of altitude or control caused by a sharp drop in speed or an excessively high angle of flight.

Streamlined: shaped to offer the least resistance to a flow of air.

Strut: straight or angled supports for landing gear and wings.

Supersonic: at a speed greater than the speed of sound.

Tail Section: the rear part of a plane.

Tail Wind: a strong movement of air having the same general direction as the course of a plane, which results in an accelerated flight.

Thrust: a forcible push or drive generated by an engine.

Trailing Edge: the rear edge of a propeller blade, wing, or tail.

Vapor Trail: the usually clear exhaust from an engine, turned visibly white by cold air.

INDEX

ABOUT
THE AUTHOR

Barbara Curry, a graduate of Western Reserve University, is currently a free-lance writer living in New York. She is the author of *Model Aircraft*, published by Franklin Watts. She has also written an adult book entitled *Okay, I'll Do It Myself*, which is a guide to repair work for the average person.